519.502

HOW

Warrington and Halton Hospitals **NHS**
NHS Foundation Trust

Knowledge & Library Service

"Bridging the Knowledge Gap"

STA   NG

D1493896

 @whhkes

Tel: 01925 662128

Email: library@whh.nhs.uk

STATISTICS

CONTENTS

4 Working with Multiple Data Sources 52

Chapter

1

INTRODUCTION

Sample Files

Most of the examples that are presented here use the data file demo.sav. This data file is a fictitious survey of several thousand people, containing basic demographic and consumer information.

If you are using the Student version, your version of demo.sav is a representative sample of the original data file, reduced to meet the 1,500-case limit. Results that you obtain using that data file will differ from the results shown here.

The sample files installed with the product can be found in the Samples subdirectory of the installation directory. There is a separate folder within the Samples subdirectory for each of the following languages: English, French, German, Italian, Japanese, Korean, Polish, Russian, Simplified Chinese, Spanish, and Traditional Chinese.

Not all sample files are available in all languages. If a sample file is not available in a language, that language folder contains an English version of the sample file.

Opening a Data File

To open a data file:
E From the menus choose:
File > Open > Data...
Alternatively, you can use the Open File button on the toolbar.

Figure 1-1

Open File toolbar button

A dialog box for opening files is displayed. 1

By default, IBM® SPSS® Statistics data files (.sav extension) are presented.

This example uses the file demo.sav.

Figure 1-2 demo.sav file in

Data Editor

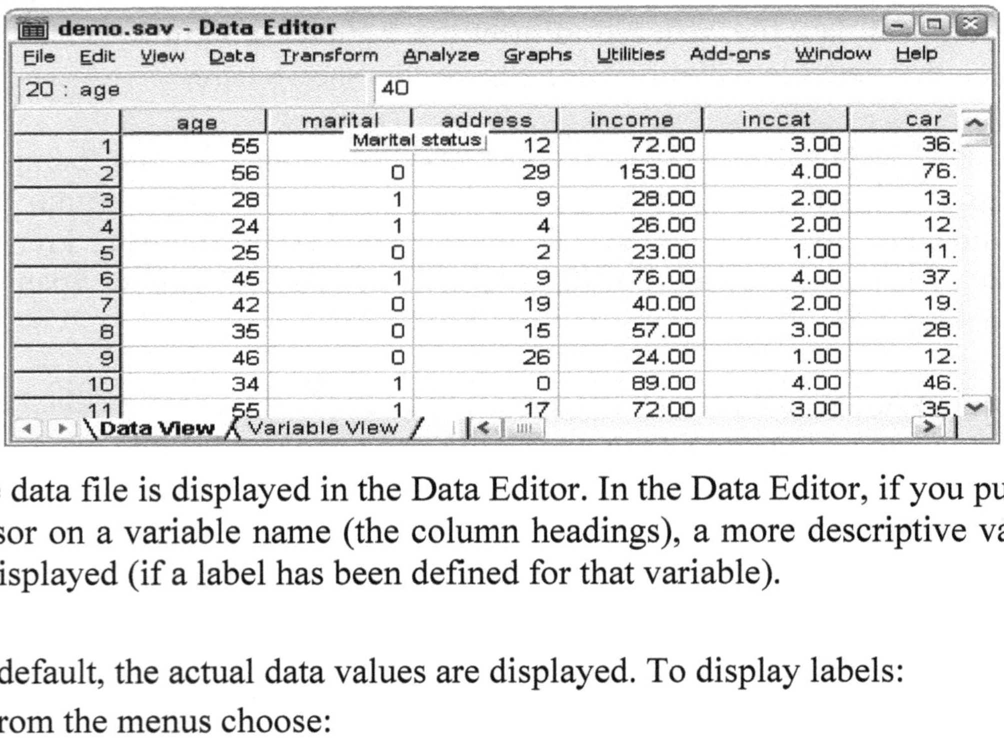

	age	marital	address	income	inccat	car
1	55	Marital status	12	72.00	3.00	36.
2	56	0	29	153.00	4.00	76.
3	28	1	9	28.00	2.00	13.
4	24	1	4	26.00	2.00	12.
5	25	0	2	23.00	1.00	11.
6	45	1	9	76.00	4.00	37.
7	42	0	19	40.00	2.00	19.
8	35	0	15	57.00	3.00	28.
9	46	0	26	24.00	1.00	12.
10	34	1	0	89.00	4.00	46.
11	55	1	17	72.00	3.00	35.

demo.sav - Data Editor — File Edit View Data Transform Analyze Graphs Utilities Add-ons Window Help — 20 : age — 40 — Data View / Variable View

The data file is displayed in the Data Editor. In the Data Editor, if you put the mouse cursor on a variable name (the column headings), a more descriptive variable label is displayed (if a label has been defined for that variable).

By default, the actual data values are displayed. To display labels:

E From the menus choose:

View > Value Labels

Alternatively, you can use the Value Labels button on the toolbar.

Figure 1-3

Value Labels button

Descriptive value labels are now displayed to make it easier to interpret the responses.

Figure 1-4

Value labels displayed in the Data Editor

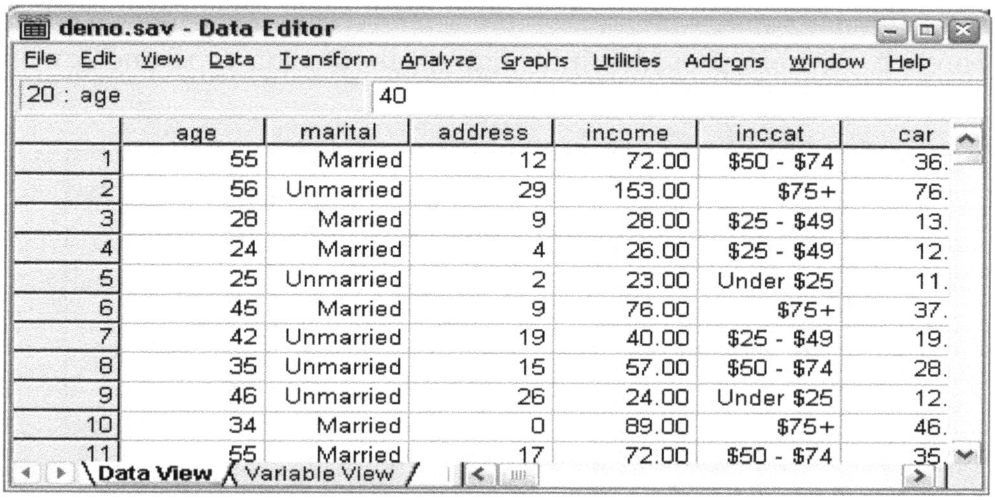

	age	marital	address	income	inccat	car
1	55	Married	12	72.00	$50 - $74	36.
2	56	Unmarried	29	153.00	$75+	76.
3	28	Married	9	28.00	$25 - $49	13.
4	24	Married	4	26.00	$25 - $49	12.
5	25	Unmarried	2	23.00	Under $25	11.
6	45	Married	9	76.00	$75+	37.
7	42	Unmarried	19	40.00	$25 - $49	19.
8	35	Unmarried	15	57.00	$50 - $74	28.
9	46	Unmarried	26	24.00	Under $25	12.
10	34	Married	0	89.00	$75+	46.
11	55	Married	17	72.00	$50 - $74	35.

demo.sav - Data Editor

File Edit View Data Transform Analyze Graphs Utilities Add-ons Window Help

20 : age   40

Data View / Variable View /

Running an Analysis

If you have any add-on options, the Analyze menu contains a list of reporting and statistical analysis categories.

We will start by creating a simple frequency table (table of counts). This example requires the Statistics Base option.

E From the menus choose:

Analyze > Descriptive Statistics > Frequencies...

The Frequencies dialog box is displayed.

Figure 1-5

Frequencies dialog box

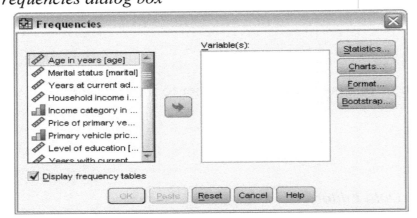

An icon next to each variable provides information about data type and level of measurement.

	Numeric	String	Date	Time
Scale (Continuous)		n/a		
Ordinal				
Nominal				

E Click the variable Income category in thousands [inccat].

Figure 1-6

Variable labels and names in the Frequencies dialog box

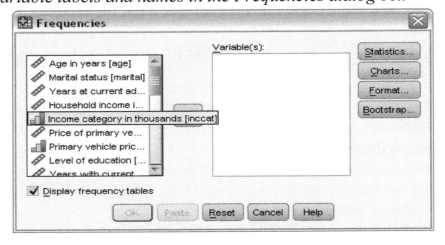

If the variable label and/or name appears truncated in the list, the complete label/name is displayed when the cursor is positioned over it. The variable name inccat is displayed in square brackets after the descriptive variable label. Income category in thousands is the variable label. If there were no variable label, only the variable name would appear in the list box.

You can resize dialog boxes just like windows, by clicking and dragging the outside borders or corners. For example, if you make the dialog box wider, the variable lists will also be wider.

Figure 1-7

Resized dialog box

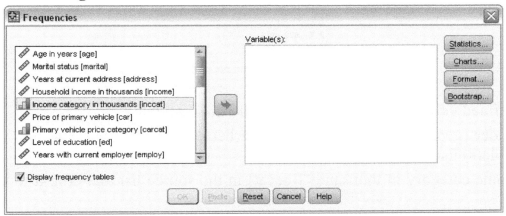

In the dialog box, you choose the variables that you want to analyze from the source list on the left and drag and drop them into the Variable (s) list on the right. The OK button, which runs the analysis, is disabled until at least one variable is placed in the Variable(s) list.

In many dialogs, you can obtain additional information by right-clicking any variable name in the list.

E Right-click Income category in thousands [inccat] and choose Variable Information.

E Click the down arrow on the Value labels drop-down list.

Figure 1-8

Defined labels for income variable

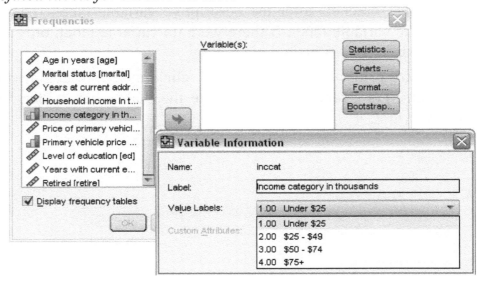

All of the defined value labels for the variable are displayed.

E Click Gender [gender] in the source variable list and drag the variable into the target Variable(s) list.

E Click Income category in thousands [inccat] in the source list and drag it to the target list.

Figure 1-9

Variables selected for analysis

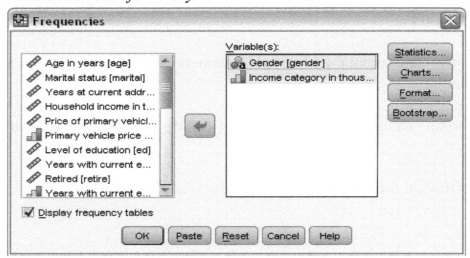

E Click OK to run the procedure.

Viewing Results

Figure 1-10

Viewer window

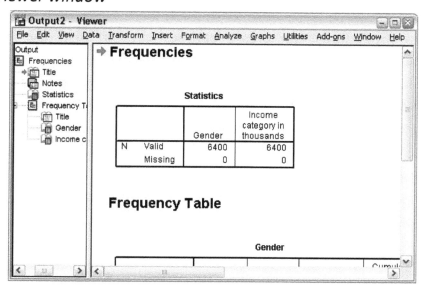

Results are displayed in the Viewer window.

You can quickly go to any item in the Viewer by selecting it in the outline pane.

E Click Income category in thousands [inccat].

Figure 1-11

Frequency table of income categories

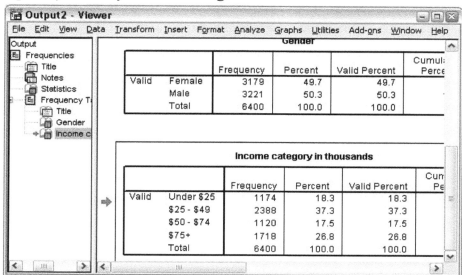

The frequency table for income categories is displayed. This frequency table shows the number and percentage of people in each income category.

Creating Charts

Although some statistical procedures can create charts, you can also use the Graphs menu to create charts.

For example, you can create a chart that shows the relationship between wireless telephone service and PDA (personal digital assistant) ownership.

E From the menus choose:

Graphs > Chart Builde.

E Click the Gallery tab (if it is not selected).

E Click Bar (if it is not selected).

E Drag the Clustered Bar icon onto the canvas, which is the large area above the Gallery.

Figure 1-12

Chart Builder dialog box

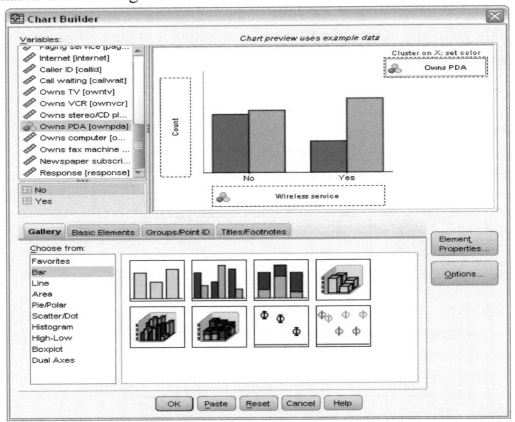

E Scroll down the Variables list, right-click Wireless service [wireless], and then choose Nominal as its measurement level.

E Drag the Wireless service [wireless] variable to the x-axis.

E Right-click Owns PDA [ownpda] and choose Nominal as its measurement level.

E Drag the Owns PDA [ownpda] variable to the cluster drop zone in the upper right corner of the canvas.

E Click OK to create the chart.

Figure 1-13

Bar chart displayed in Viewer window

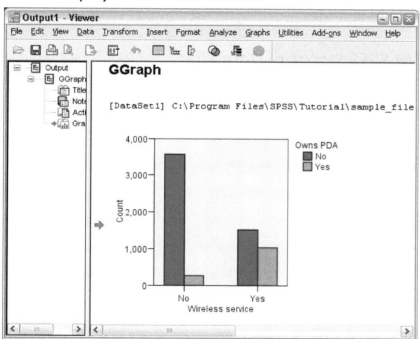

The bar chart is displayed in the Viewer. The chart shows that people with wireless phone service are far more likely to have PDAs than people without wireless service.

You can edit charts and tables by double-clicking them in the contents pane of the Viewer window, and you can copy and paste your results into other applications. Those topics will be covered later.

Chapter

2

READING DATA

Data can be entered directly, or it can be imported from a number of different sources. The processes for reading data stored in IBM® SPSS® Statistics data files; spreadsheet applications, such as Microsoft Excel; database applications, such as Microsoft Access; and text files are all discussed in this chapter.

Basic Structure of IBM SPSS Statistics Data Files

Figure 2-1

Data Editor

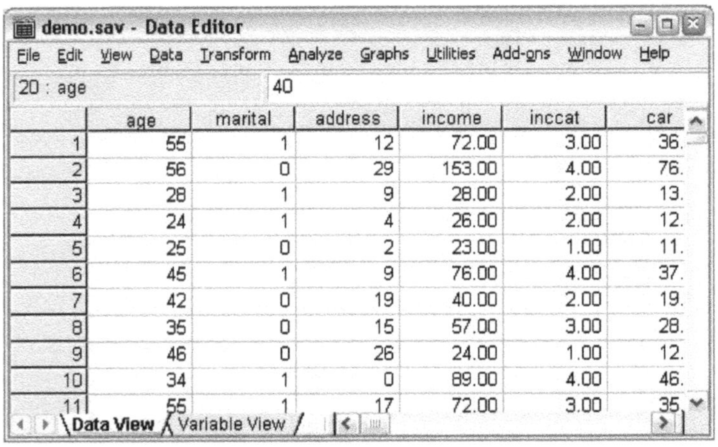

	age	marital	address	income	inccat	car
1	55	1	12	72.00	3.00	36.
2	56	0	29	153.00	4.00	76.
3	28	1	9	28.00	2.00	13.
4	24	1	4	26.00	2.00	12.
5	25	0	2	23.00	1.00	11.
6	45	1	9	76.00	4.00	37.
7	42	0	19	40.00	2.00	19.
8	35	0	15	57.00	3.00	28.
9	46	0	26	24.00	1.00	12.
10	34	1	0	89.00	4.00	46.
11	55	1	17	72.00	3.00	35.

IBM® SPSS® Statistics data files are organized by cases (rows) and variables (columns). In this data file, cases represent individual respondents to a survey. Variables represent responses to each question asked in the survey.

Reading IBM SPSS Statistics Data Files

IBM® SPSS® Statistics data files, which have a .sav file extension, contain your saved data. To open demo.sav, an example file installed with the product:

E From the menus choose:

File > Open > Data...

E Browse to and open demo.sav.

The data are now displayed in the Data Editor.

Figure 2-2

Opened data file

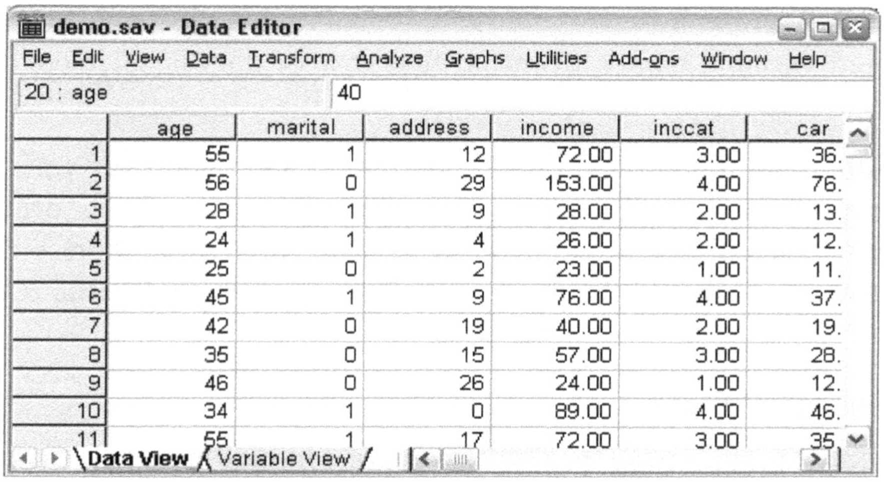

Reading Data from Spreadsheets

Rather than typing all of your data directly into the Data Editor, you can read data from applications such as Microsoft Excel. You can also read column headings as variable names.

E From the menus choose:

File > Open > Data...

E Select Excel (*.xls) as the file type you want to view.

E Open demo.xls.

The Opening Excel Data Source dialog box is displayed, allowing you to specify whether variable names are to be included in the spreadsheet, as well as the cells that you want to import. In Excel 95 or later, you can also specify which worksheets you want to import.

Figure 2-3

Opening Excel Data Source dialog box

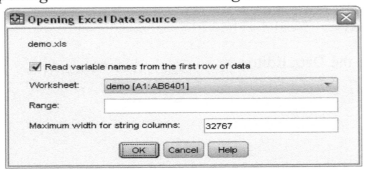

E Make sure that Read variable names from the first row of data is selected. This option reads column headings as variable names.

If the column headings do not conform to the IBM® SPSS® Statistics variable-naming rules, they are converted into valid variable names and the original column headings are saved as variable labels. If you want to import only a portion of the spreadsheet, specify the range of cells to be imported in the Range text box.

E Click OK to read the Excel file.

The data now appear in the Data Editor, with the column headings used as variable names. Since variable names can't contain spaces, the spaces from the original column headings have been removed. For example, Marital status in the Excel file becomes the variable Maritalstatus. The original column heading is retained as a variable label.

Figure 2-4

Imported Excel data

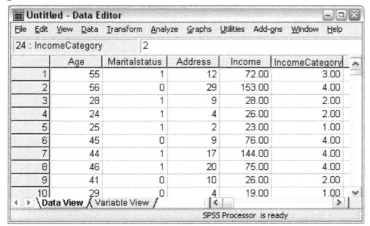

Reading Data from a Database

Data from database sources are easily imported using the Database Wizard. Any database that uses ODBC (Open Database Connectivity) drivers can be read directly after the drivers are installed. ODBC drivers for many database formats are supplied on the installation CD. Additional drivers can be obtained from third-party vendors. One of the most common database applications, Microsoft Access, is discussed in this example.

Note: This example is specific to Microsoft Windows and requires an ODBC driver for Access. The steps are similar on other platforms but may require a third-party ODBC driver for Access.

E From the menus choose:

File > Open Database > New Query...

Figure 2-5

Database Wizard Welcome dialog box

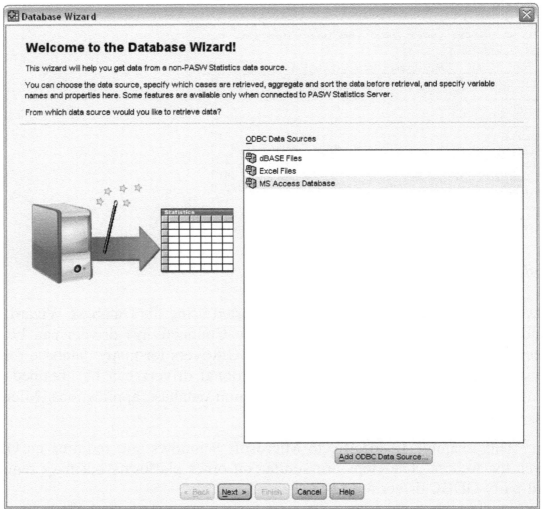

E Select MS Access Database from the list of data sources and click Next.

Note: Depending on your installation, you may also see a list of OLEDB data sources on the left side of the wizard (Windows operating systems only), but this example uses the list of ODBC data sources displayed on the right side.

Figure 2-6

ODBC Driver Login dialog box

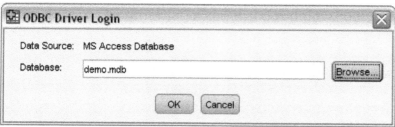

E Click Browse to navigate to the Access database file that you want to open.

E *Open demo.mdb.*

E Click OK in the login dialog box.

In the next step, you can specify the tables and variables that you want to import.

Figure 2-7

Select Data step

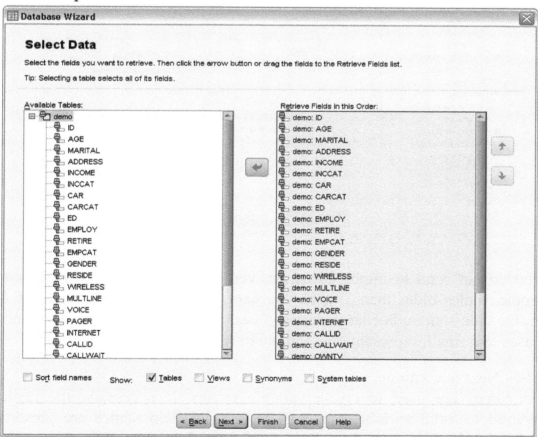

E Drag the entire demo table to the Retrieve Fields In This Order list.

E Click Next.

In the next step, you select which records (cases) to import.

Figure 2-8

Limit Retrieved Cases step

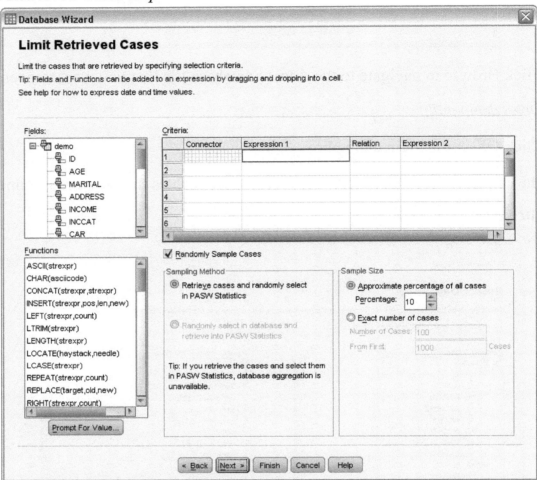

If you do not want to import all cases, you can import a subset of cases (for example, males older than 30), or you can import a random sample of cases from the data source. For large data sources, you may want to limit the number of cases to a small, representative sample to reduce the processing time.

E Click Next to continue.

Field names are used to create variable names. If necessary, the names are converted to valid variable names. The original field names are preserved as variable labels. You can also change the variable names before importing the database.

Figure 2-9

Define Variables step

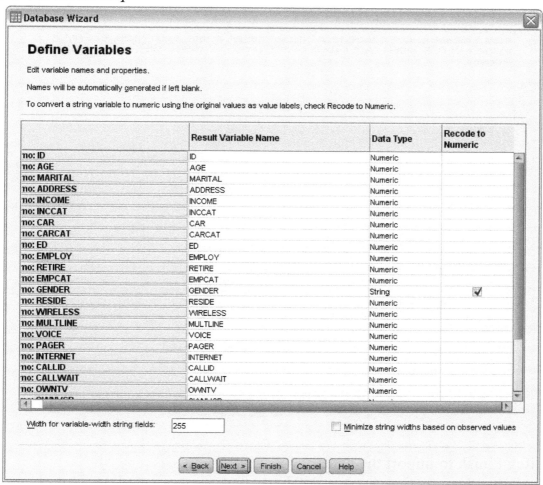

E Click the Recode to Numeric cell in the Gender field. This option converts string variables to integer variables and retains the original value as the value label for the new variable.

E Click Next to continue.

The SQL statement created from your selections in the Database Wizard appears in the Results step. This statement can be executed now or saved to a file for later use.

Figure 2-10

Results step

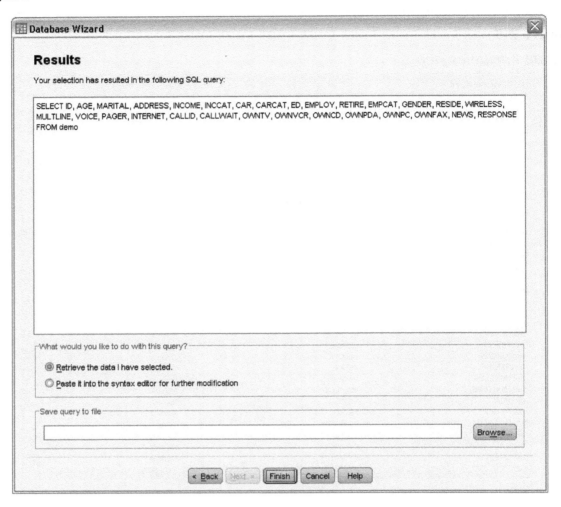

E Click Finish to import the data.

All of the data in the Access database that you selected to import are now available in the Data Editor.

Figure 2-11

Data imported from an Access database

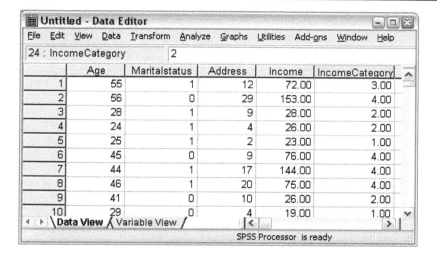

Reading Data from a Text File

Text files are another common source of data. Many spreadsheet programs and databases can save their contents in one of many text file formats. Comma- or tab-delimited files refer to rows of data that use commas or tabs to indicate each variable. In the this example, the data are tab delimited.

E From the menus choose:

File > Read Text Data...

E Select Text (*.txt) as the file type you want to view.

E Open demo.txt.

The Text Import Wizard guides you through the process of defining how the specified text file should be interpreted.

Figure 2-12
Text Import Wizard: Step 1 of 6

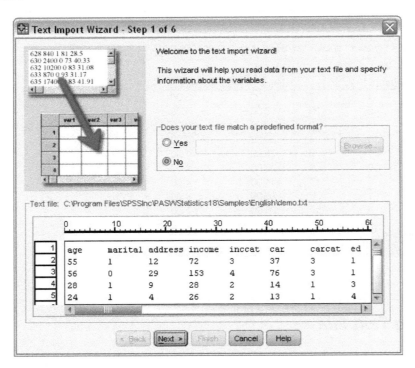

E In Step 1, you can choose a predefined format or create a new format in the wizard. Select No to indicate that a new format should be created.

E Click Next to continue.

As stated earlier, this file uses tab-delimited formatting. Also, the variable names are defined on the top line of this file.

Figure 2-13

Text Import Wizard: Step 2 of 6

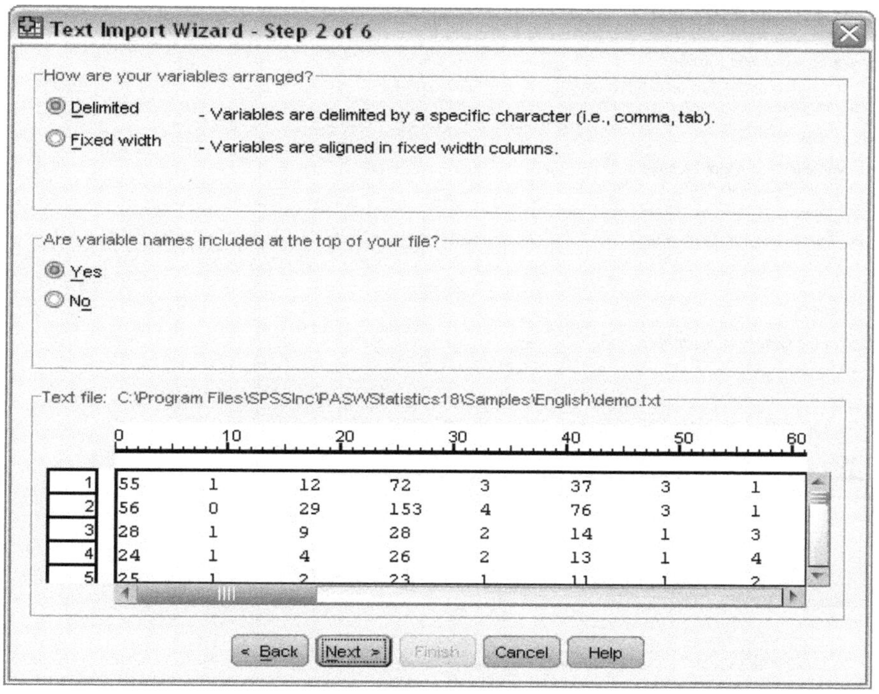

E Select Delimited to indicate that the data use a delimited formatting structure.

E Select Yes to indicate that variable names should be read from the top of the file.

E Click Next to continue.

E Type 2 in the top section of next dialog box to indicate that the first row of data starts on the second line of the text file.

Figure 2-14

Text Import Wizard: Step 3 of 6

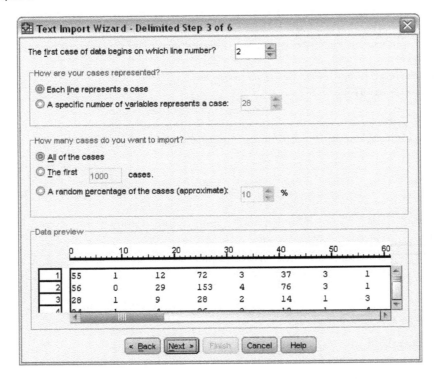

E Keep the default values for the remainder of this dialog box, and click Next to continue.

The Data preview in Step 4 provides you with a quick way to ensure that your data are being adequately read.

Figure 2-15

Text Import Wizard: Step 4 of 6

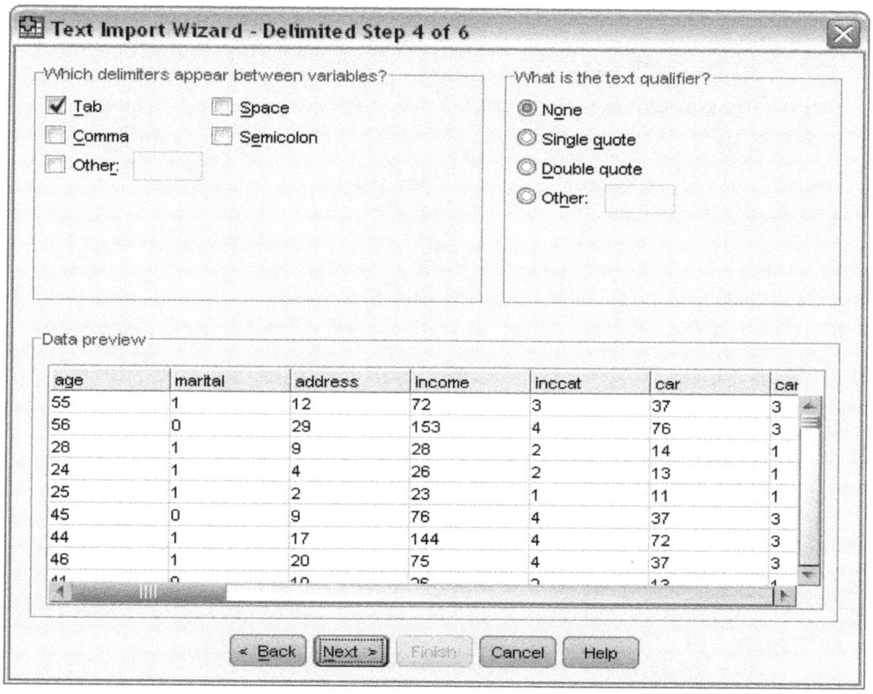

E Select Tab and deselect the other options.

E Click Next to continue.

Because the variable names may have been truncated to fit formatting requirements, this dialog box gives you the opportunity to edit any undesirable names.

Figure 2-16

Text Import Wizard: Step 5 of 6

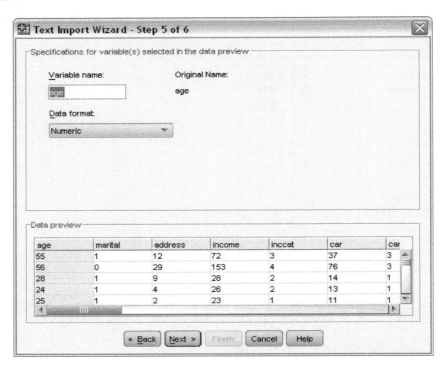

Data types can be defined here as well. For example, it's safe to assume that the income variable is meant to contain a certain dollar amount.

To change a data type:

E Under Data preview, select the variable you want to change, which is Income in this case.

E Select Dollar from the Data format drop-down list.

Figure 2-17

Change the data type

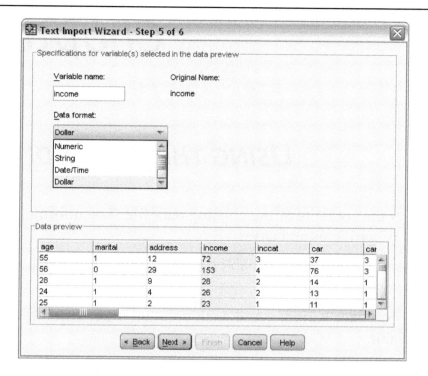

E Click Next to continue.

Figure 2-18

Text Import Wizard: Step 6 of 6

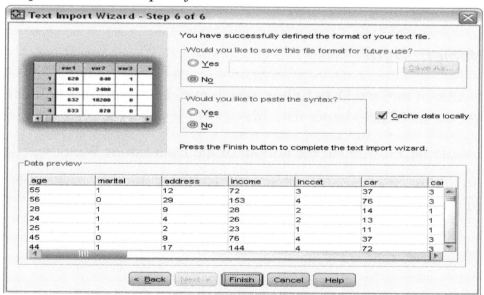

E Leave the default selections in this dialog box, and click Finish to import the data.

Chapter 3

USING THE DATA EDITOR

The Data Editor Displays the contents of the existing data file. The information in the Data Editor consists of variables and cases.

In Data View, columns represent variables, and rows represent cases (observations).

In Variable View, each row is a variable, and each column is an attribute that is associated with that variable.

Variables are used to represent the different type's of data that you have compiled. A common analogy is that of a survey. The response to each question on a survey is equivalent to a variable. Variables come in many different types, including numbers, strings, currency, and dates.

Entering Numeric Data

Data can be entered into the Data Editor, which may be useful for small data files or for making minor edits to larger data files.

E Click the Variable View tab at the bottom of the Data Editor Window.

You need to define the variables that will be used. In this case, only three variables are needed: *age, marital status, and income*.

Figure 3-1

Variable names in Variable View

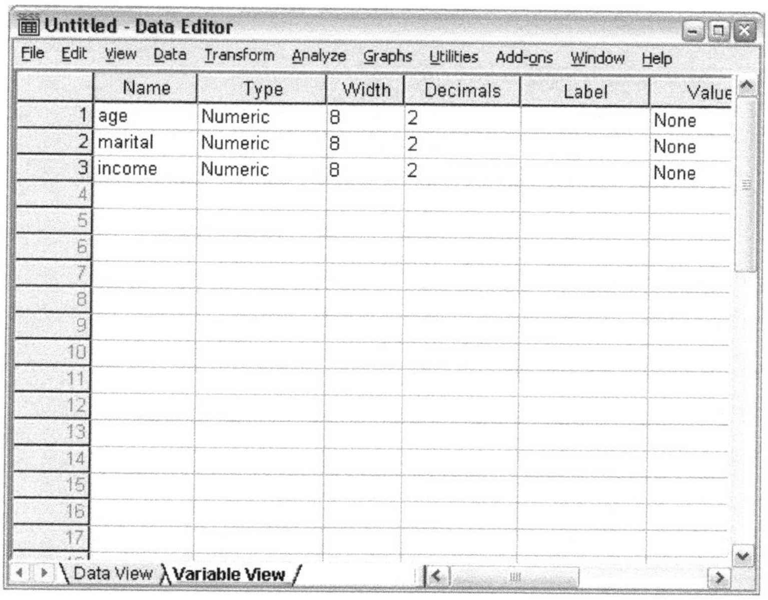

E In the first row of the first column, type age.

E In the second row, type marital.

E In the third row, type income.

New variables are automatically given a Numeric data type.

If you don't enter variable names, unique names are automatically created. However, these names are not descriptive and are not recommended for large data files.

E Click the Data View tab to continue entering the data.

The names that you entered in Variable View are now the headings for the first three columns in Data View.

Begin entering data in the first row, starting at the first column.

Figure 3-2

Values entered in Data View

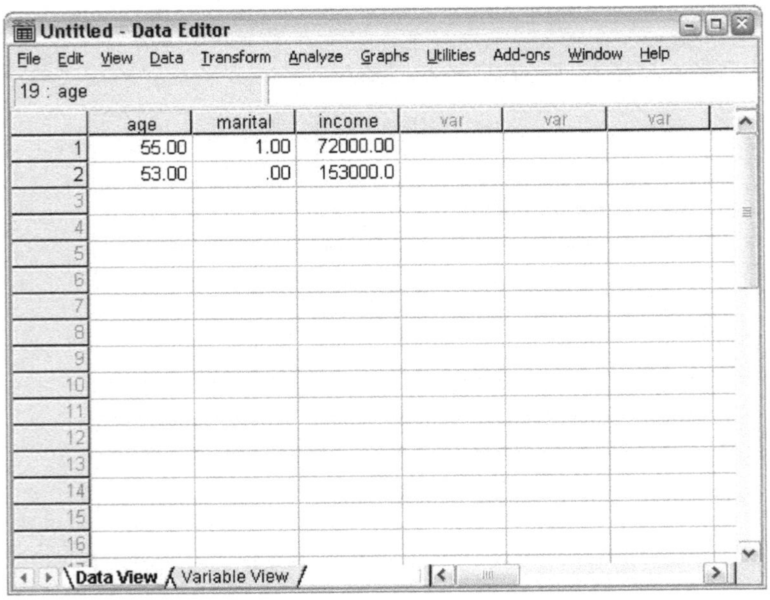

E In the age column, type 55.

E In the marital column, type 1.

E In the income column, type 72000.

E Move the cursor to the second row of the first column to add the next subject's data.

E In the age column, type 53.

E In the marital column, type 0.

E In the income column, type 153000.

Currently, the age and marital columns display decimal points, even though their values are intended to be integers. To hide the decimal points in these variables:

E Click the Variable View tab at the bottom of the Data Editor window.

E In the Decimals column of the age row, type 0 to hide the decimal.

E In the Decimals column of the marital row, type 0 to hide the decimal.

Figure 3-3

Updated decimal property for age and marital

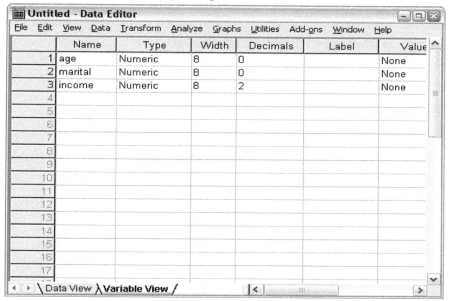

Entering String Data

Non-numeric data, such as strings of text, can also be entered into the Data Editor.

E Click the Variable View tab at the bottom of the Data Editor Window.

E In the first cell of the first empty row, type sex for the variable name.

E Click the Type cell next to your entry.

E Click the button on the right side of the Type cell to open the Variable Type dialog box.

Figure 3-4

Button shown in Type cell for sex

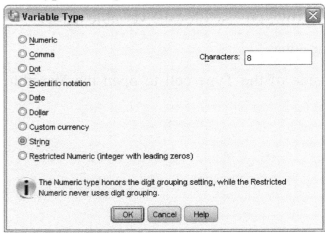

E Select String to specify the variable type.

E Click OK to save your selection and return to the Data Editor.

Figure 3-5

Variable Type dialog box

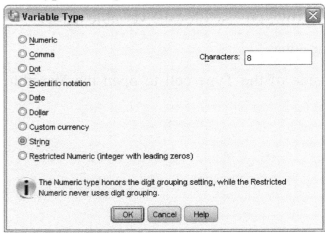

Defining Data

In addition to defining data types, you can also define descriptive variable labels and value labels for variable names and data values. These descriptive labels are used in statistical reports and charts.

Adding Variable Labels

Labels are meant to provide descriptions of variables. These descriptions are often longer versions of variable names. Labels can be up to 255 bytes. These labels are used in your output to identify the different variables.

E Click the Variable View tab at the bottom of the Data Editor window.

E In the Label column of the age row, type Respondent's Age.

E In the Label column of the marital row, type Marital Status.

E In the Label column of the income row, type Household Income.

E In the Label column of the sex row, type Gender.

Figure 3-6

Variable labels entered in Variable View

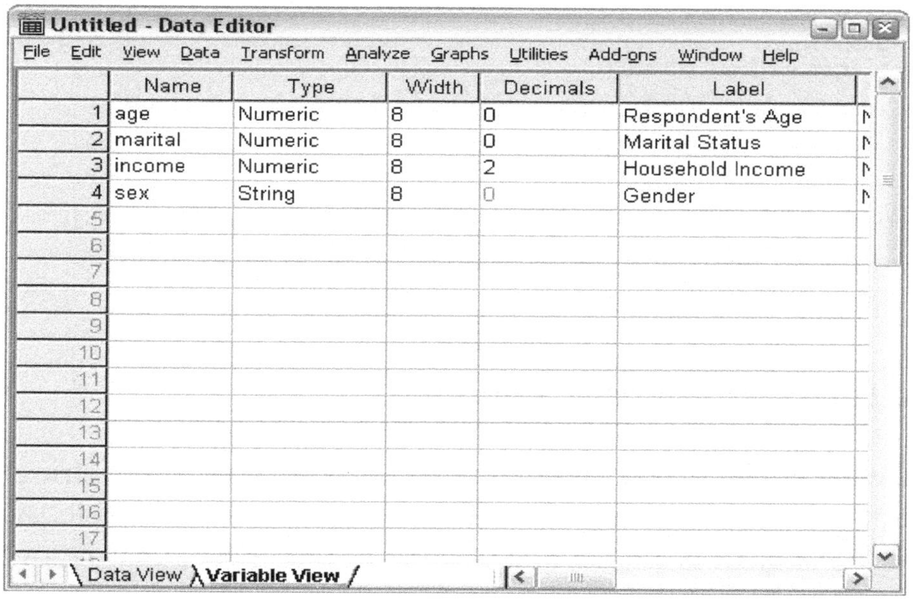

Changing Variable Type and Format

The Type column displays the current data type for each variable. The most common data types are numeric and string, but many other formats are supported. In the current data file, the income variable is defined as a numeric type.

E. Click the Type cell for the income row, and then click the button on the right side of the cell to open the Variable Type dialog box.

E. Select Dollar.

Figure 3-7

Variable Type dialog box

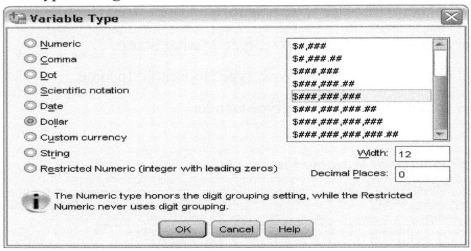

The formatting options for the currently selected data type are displayed.
E For the format of the currency in this example, select $###,###,###.
E Click OK to save your changes.

Adding Value Labels for Numeric Variables

Value labels provide a method for mapping your variable values to a string label. In this example, there are two acceptable values for the marital variable. A value of 0 means that the subject is single, and a value of one means that he or she is married.

EClick the Values cell for the marital row and then click the button on the right side of the cell to open the Value Labels dialog box.

The **value** is the actual numeric value.

The **value label** is the string label that is applied to the specified numeric value.

E Type 0 in the Value field.

E Type Single in the Label field.

E Click Add to add this label to the list.

Figure 3-8

Value Labels dialog box

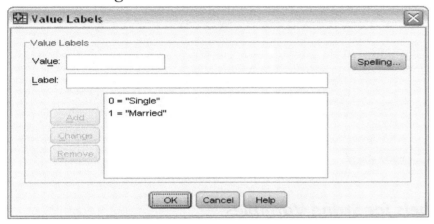

E Type 1 in the Value field, and type Married in the Label field.

E Click Add, and then click OK to save your changes and return to the Data Editor.

These labels can also be displayed in Data View, which can make your data more readable.

E Click the Data View tab at the bottom of the Data Editor window.

E From the menus choose:

View > Value Labels

The labels are now displayed in a list when you enter values in the Data Editor. This setup has the benefit of suggesting a valid response and providing a more descriptive answer.

If the Value Labels menu item is already active (with a check mark next to it), choosing Value Labels again will turn off the display of value labels.

Figure 3-9

Value labels displayed in Data View

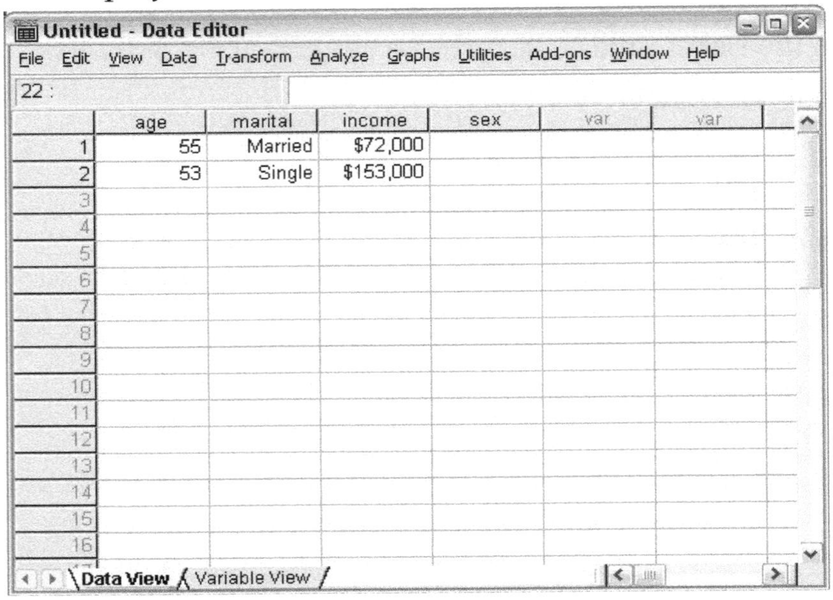

Adding Value Labels for String Variables

String variables may require value labels as well. For example, your data may use single letters, M or F, to identify the sex of the subject. Value labels can be used to specify that M stands for Male and F stands for Female.

E Click the Variable View tab at the bottom of the Data Editor window.

E Click the Values cell in the sex row, and then click the button on the right side of the cell to open the Value Labels dialog box.

E Type F in the Value field, and then type Female in the Label field.

E Click Add to add this label to your data file.

Figure 3-10

Value Labels dialog box

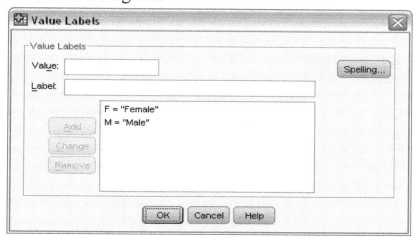

E Type M in the Value field, and type Male in the Label field.

E Click Add, and then click OK to save your changes and return to the Data Editor.

Because string values are case sensitive; you should be consistent. A lowercase m is not the same as an uppercase M.

Using Value Labels for Data Entry

You can use value labels for data entry.

E Click the Data View tab at the bottom of the Data Editor window.

E In the first row, select the cell for sex.

E Click the button on the right side of the cell, and then choose Male from the drop-down list.

E In the second row, select the cell for sex.

Click the button on the right side of the cell, and then choose Female from the drop-down list.

Figure 3-11

Using variable labels to select values

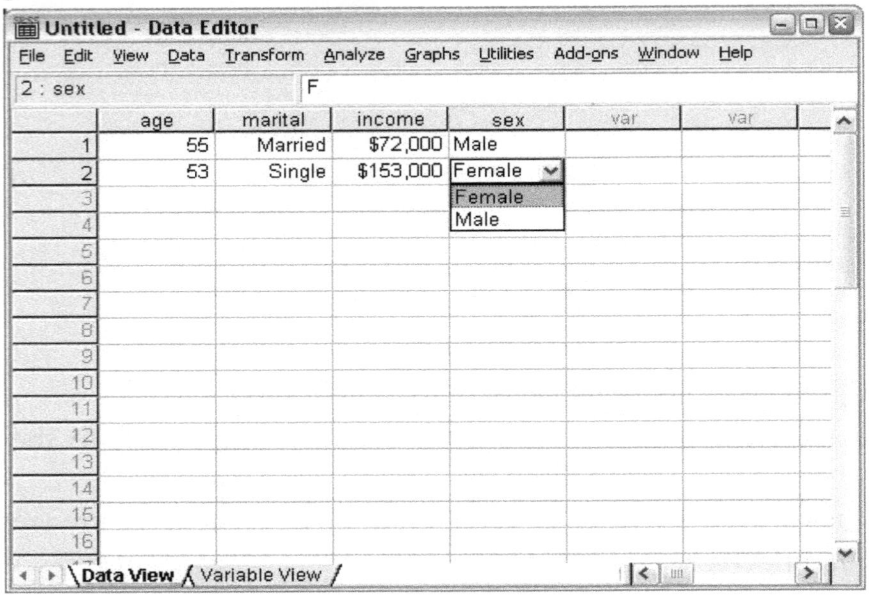

Only defined values are listed, which ensures that the entered data are in a format that you expect.

Handling Missing Data

Missing or invalid data are generally too common to ignore. Survey respondents may refuse to answer certain questions, may not know the answer, or may answer in an unexpected format. If you don't filter or identify these data, your analysis may not provide accurate results.

For numeric data, empty data fields or fields containing invalid entries are converted to system-missing, which is identifiable by a single period.

Figure 3-12

Missing values displayed as periods

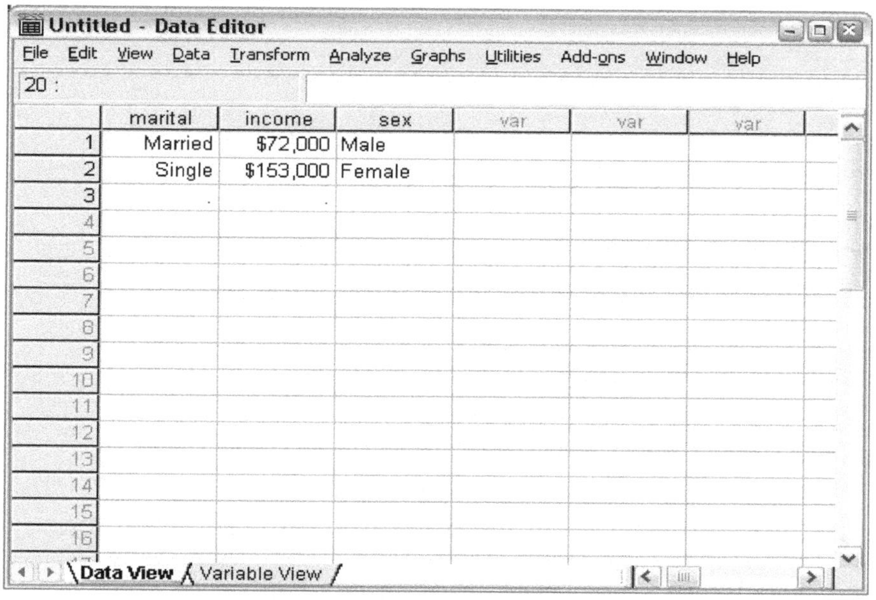

The reason a value is missing may be important to your analysis. For example, you may find it useful to distinguish between those respondents who refused to answer a question and those respondents who didn't answer a question because it was not applicable.

Missing Values for a Numeric Variable

E Click the Variable View tab at the bottom of the Data Editor window.

E Click the Missing cell in the age row, and then click the button on the right side of the cell to open the Missing Values dialog box.

In this dialog box, you can specify up to three distinct missing values, or you can specify a range of values plus one additional discrete value.

Figure 3-13

Missing Values dialog box

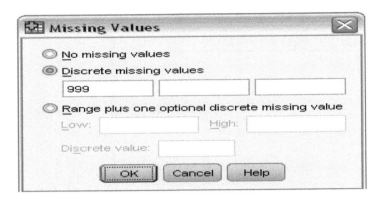

Select Discrete missing values.

E Type 999 in the first text box and leave the other two text boxes empty.

E Click OK to save your changes and return to the Data Editor.

Now that the missing data value has been added, a label can be applied to that value.

E Click the Values cell in the age row and then click the button on the right side of the cell to open the Value Labels dialog box.

E Type 999 in the Value field.

E Type No Response in the Label field.

Figure 3-14

Value Labels dialog box

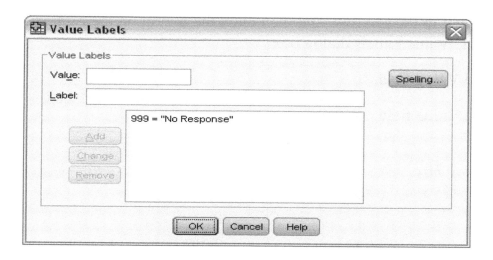

E Click Add to add this label to your data file.

E Click OK to save your changes and return to the Data Editor.

Missing Values for a String Variable

Missing values for string variables are handled similarly to the missing values for numeric variables. However, unlike numeric variables, empty fields in string variables are not designated as system-missing. Rather, they are interpreted as an empty string.

E Click the Variable View tab at the bottom of the Data Editor window.

E Click the Missing cell in the sex row, and then click the button on the right side of the cell to open the Missing Values dialog box.

E Select Discrete missing values.

E Type NR in the first text box.

Missing values for string variables are case sensitive. So, a value of nr is not treated as a missing value.

Click OK to save your changes and return to the Data Editor.

Now you can add a label for the missing value.

E Click the Values cell in the sex row, and then click the button on the right side of the cell to open the Value Labels dialog box.

E Type NR in the Value field.

E Type NR in the Value field.

Figure 3-15

Value Labels dialog box

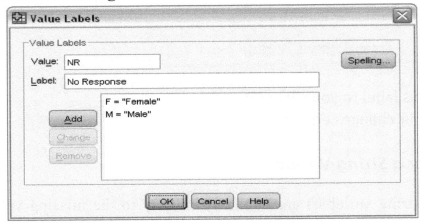

E Click Add to add this label to your project.
E Click OK to save your changes and return to the Data Editor.

Copying and Pasting Variable Attributes

After you've defined variable attributes for a variable, you can copy these attributes and apply them to other variables.
In Variable View, type agewed in the first cell of the first empty row.

Figure 3-16
Agewed variable in Variable View

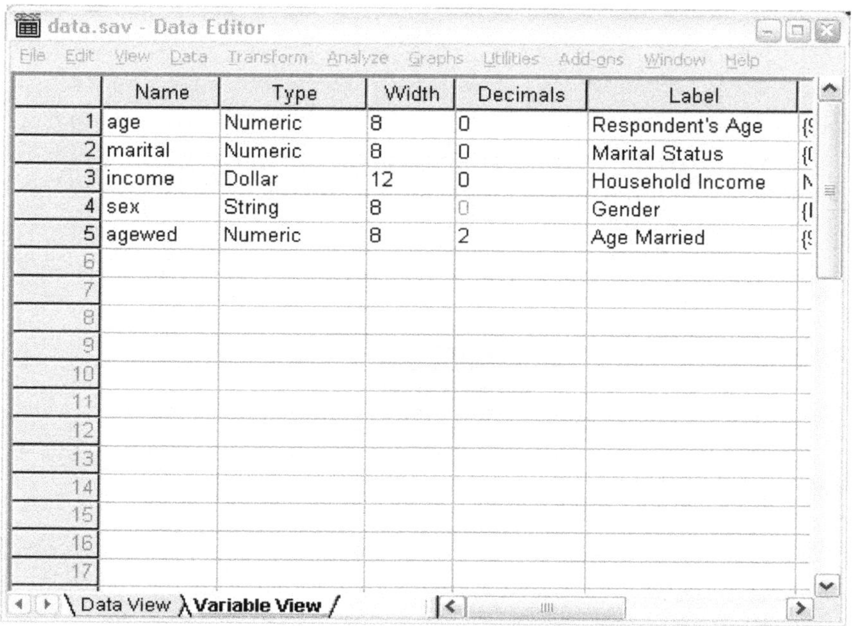

E In the Label column, type Age Married.

E Click the Values cell in the age row.

E From the menus choose:

Edit > Copy

E Click the Values cell in the agewed row.

E From the menus choose:

Edit > Paste

The defined values from the age variable are now applied to the agewed variable.

To apply the attribute to multiple variables, simply select multiple target cells (click and drag down the column).

Figure 3-17

Multiple cells selected

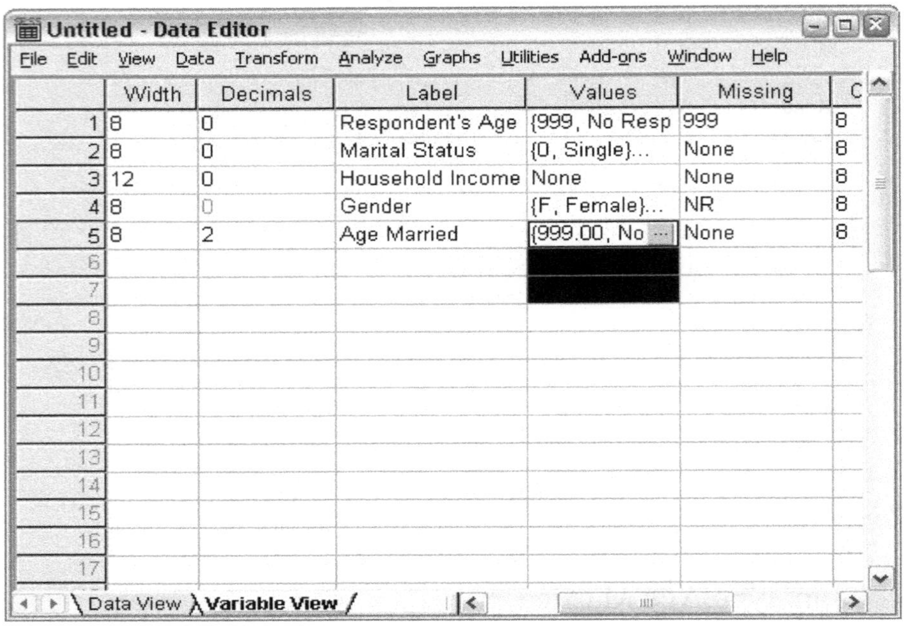

When you paste the attribute, it is applied to all of the chosen cells.
New variables are automatically created if you paste the values into empty rows.

To copy all attributes from one variable to another variable:
E Click the row number in the marital row.

Figure 3-18

Selected row

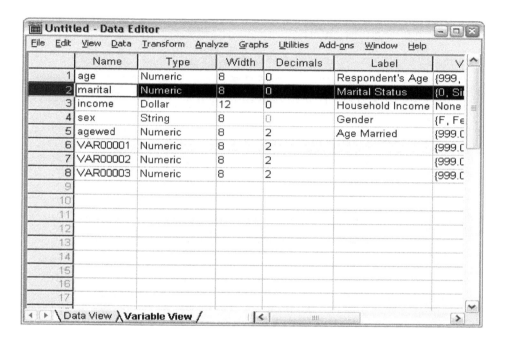

E From the menus choose:

Edit > Copy

E Click the row number of the first empty row.

E From the menus choose:

Edit > Paste
All attributes of the marital variable are applied to the new variable.

Figure 3-19

All values pasted into a row

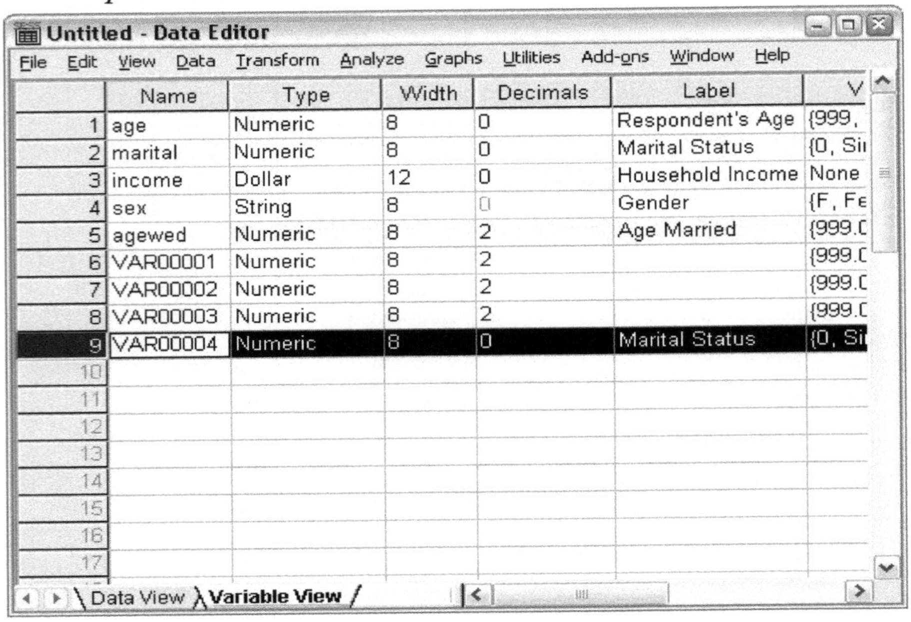

Defining Variable Properties for Categorical Variables

For categorical (nominal, ordinal) data, you can use Define Variable Properties to define value labels and other variable properties. The Define Variable Properties process:

④ Scans the actual data values and lists all unique data values for each selected variable.

④ Identifies unlabeled values and provides an "auto-label" feature.

Provides the ability to copy defined value labels from another variable to the selected variable or from the selected variable to additional variables.

This example uses the data file demo.sav. This data file already has defined value labels, so we will enter a value for which there is no defined value label.

E In Data View of the Data Editor, click the first data cell for the variable ownpc (you may have to scroll to the right), and then enter 99.

E From the menus choose:

Data > Define Variable Properties...

Figure 3-20
Initial Define Variable Properties dialog box

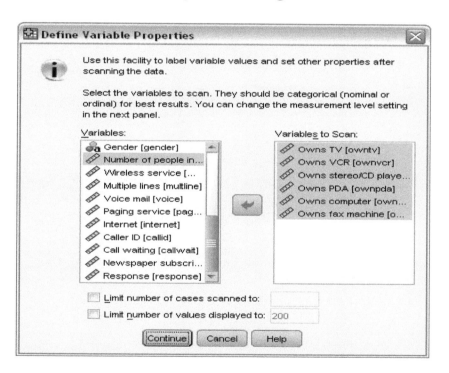

In the initial Define Variable Properties dialog box, you select the nominal or ordinal variables for which you want to define value labels and other properties.

E Drag and drop Owns TV [owntv] through Owns fax machine [ownfax] into the Variables to

Scan list.

You might notice that the measurement level icons for all of the selected variables indicate that they are scale variables, not categorical variables. All of the selected variables in this example are really categorical variables that use the numeric values 0 and 1 to stand for No and Yes, respectively—and one of the variable properties that we'll change with Define Variable Properties is the measurement level.

E Click Continue.

Figure 3-*21*

Define Variable Properties main dialog box

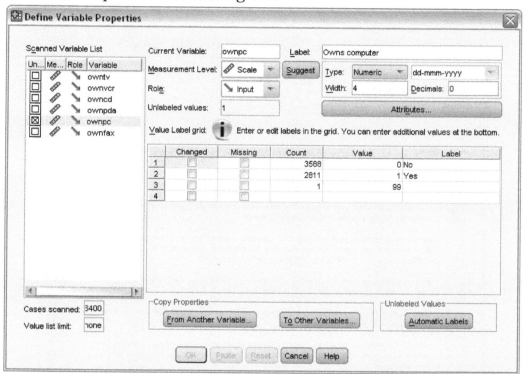

E In the Scanned Variable List, select ownpc.

The current level of measurement for the selected variable is scale. You can change the measurement level by selecting a level from the drop-down list, or you can let Define Variable Properties suggest a measurement level.

E Click Suggest.

The Suggest Measurement Level dialog box is displayed.

Figure *3-22*

Suggest Measurement Level dialog box

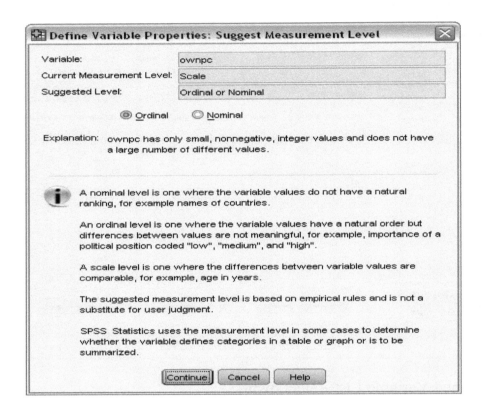

Because the variable doesn't have very many different values and all of the scanned cases contain integer values, the proper measurement level is probably ordinal or nominal.

E Select Ordinal, and then click Continue.

The measurement level for the selected variable is now ordinal.

The Value Label grid displays all of the unique data values for the selected variable, any defined value labels for these values and the number of times (count) that each value occurs in the scanned cases.

The value that we entered in Data View, 99, is displayed in the grid. The count is only one because we changed the value for only one case, and the Label column is empty because we haven't defined a value label for 99 yet. An X in the first column of the Scanned Variable List also indicates that the selected variable has at least one observed value without a defined value label.

E In the Label column for the value of 99, enter No answer.

E-Check the box in the Missing column for the value 99 to identify the value 99 as user-missing. Data values that are specified as user-missing are flagged for special treatment and are excluded from most calculations.

Figure 3-23

New variable properties defined for own pc

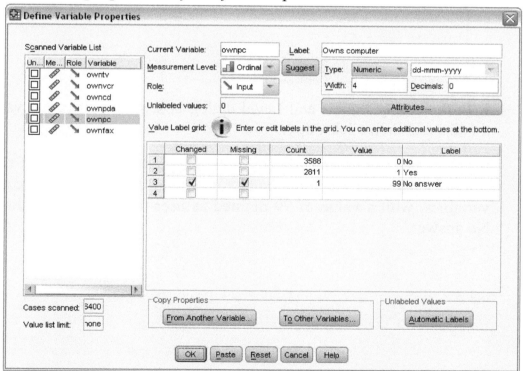

Before we complete the job of modifying the variable properties for ownpc, let's apply the same measurement level, value labels, and missing values definitions to the other variables in the list.

E In the Copy Properties area, click To Other Variables.

Figure *3-24*
Apply Labels and Level dialog box

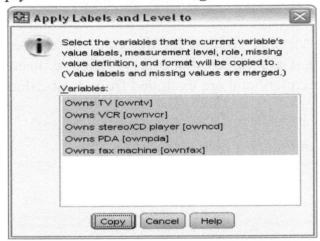

E In the Apply Labels and Level dialog box, select all of the variables in the list, and then click Copy.

If you select any other variable in the Scanned Variable List of the Define Variable Properties main dialog box now, you'll see that they are all ordinal variables, with a value of 99 defined as user-missing and a value label of No answer.

Figure 3-25

New variable properties defined for ownfax

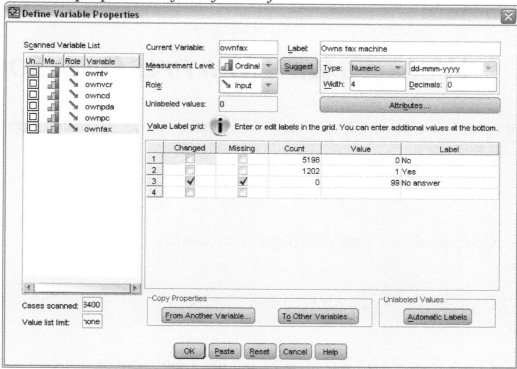

E Click OK to save all of the variable properties that you have defined.

Chapter 4

WORKING WITH MULTIPLE DATA SOURCE

Starting with version 14.0, multiple data sources can be open at the same time, making it easier to:

- Switch back and forth between data sources.

- Compare the contents of different data sources.

- Copy and paste data between data sources.

- Create multiple subsets of cases and/or variables for analysis.

Merge multiple data sources from various data formats (for example, spreadsheet, database, text data) without saving each data source first.

Basic Handling of Multiple Data Sources

Figure 4-1

Two data sources open at same time

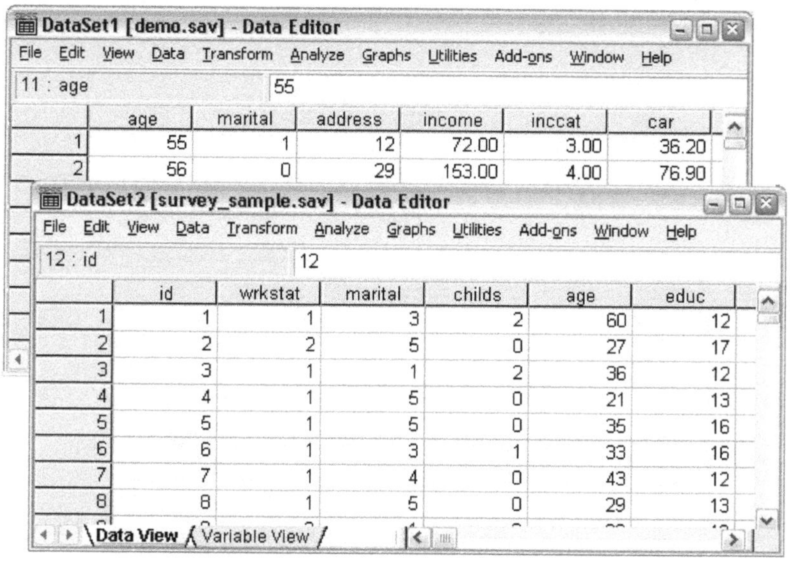

By default, each data source that you open is displayed in a new Data Editor window.

④   Any previously open data sources remain open and available for further use.

④   When you first open a data source, it automatically becomes the active dataset.

④   You can change the active dataset simply by clicking anywhere in the Data Editor window of the data source that you want to use or by selecting the Data Editor window for that data source from the Window menu.

④ Only the variables in the active dataset are available for analysis.

Figure 4-2

Variable list containing variables in the active dataset

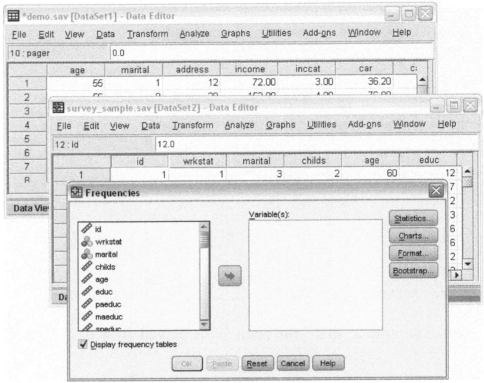

④ You cannot change the active dataset when any dialog box that accesses the data is open (including all dialog boxes that display variable lists).

④ At least one, Data Editor window must be open during a session. When you close the last open Data Editor window, IBM® SPSS® Statistics automatically shuts down, prompting you to save changes first.

Working with Multiple Datasets in Command Syntax

If you use command syntax to open data sources (for example, GET FILE, GET DATA), you need to use the DATASET NAME command to name each dataset explicitly in order to have more than one data source open at the same time.

When working with command syntax, the active dataset name is displayed on the toolbar of the syntax window. All of the following actions can change the active dataset:

④   Use the DATASET ACTIVATE command.

④   Click anywhere in the Data Editor window of a dataset.

④   Select a dataset name from the toolbar in the syntax window.

Figure 4-3

Open datasets displayed on syntax window toolbar

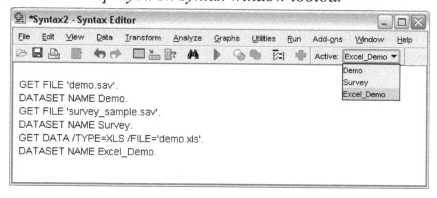

Copying and Pasting Information between Datasets

You can copy both data and variable definition attributes from one dataset to another dataset in basically the same way that you copy and paste information within a single data file.

④   Copying and pasting selected data cells in Data View pastes only the data values, with no variable definition attributes.

④   Copying and pasting an entire variable in Data View by selecting the variable name at the top of the column pastes all of the data and all of the variable definition attributes for that variable.

④   Copying and pasting variable definition attributes or entire variables in Variable View pastes the selected attributes (or the entire variable definition) but does not paste any data values.

Renaming Datasets

When you open a data source through the menus and dialog boxes, each data source is automatically assigned a dataset name of DataSetn, where n is a sequential integer value, and when you open a data source using command syntax, no dataset name is assigned unless you explicitly specify one with DATASET NAME. To provide more descriptive dataset names:

E From the menus in the Data Editor window for the dataset whose name you want to change choose:

File > Rename Dataset...

E Enter a new dataset name that conforms to variable naming rules.

Suppressing Multiple Datasets

If you prefer to have only one dataset available at a time and want to suppress the multiple dataset feature:

E From the menus choose:

Edit > Options...
E Click the General tab.

Select (check) Open only one dataset at a time.

Other Books by Andrei Besedin

Learn-Miscrosoft-Publisher-Software-Quickly

How-Learn-QuickBooks-Accounting-Quickly

How-Learn-Microsoft-Server-Quickly

How-Learn-Microsoft-Visio-Quickly

Secrets-Access-Database-Development-Programming

Powerful-Excel-Conditional-Formatting-Techniques

Top-Numerical-Methods-MATLAB-Beginners

Secrets-Access-Database-Development-Programming

Secrets-Project-Management-Using-Microsoft

Learn-Microsoft-Access-Programming-Quickly

Secrets-Building-Successful-Business-Rural

Most-Powerful-Excel-Functions-Formulas

Secrets-Statistical-Analysis-Management-Science

How-Learn-Quickbooks-Accounting-Quickly

Develop-microsoft-keyboarding-document-processing

How-Learn-Microsoft-VISIO-Quickly

Secrets-Access-Accounting

150-Most-Powerful-Excel-Shortcuts

Learn-Microsoft-Office-Outlook-Quickly

MS-Excel-Bible-Quality-Package

Secrets-Business-Math-Using-Excel

Top-Secrets-Excel-Dashboards-Save

learn-Microsoft-Office-Powerpoint-Quickly

MOST-POWERFUL-FEATURES-PIVOT-TABLES

Most-Powerful-Excel-Functions-Formulas

Most-Powerful-Features-Pivot-Tables

Top-Excel-VBA-Simulations-Investments

Powerful-Excel-Conditional-Formatting-Techniques

Secrets-Lookup-Become-Productive-Vlookup

ORDERS-MEDALS-USSR

Dash-diet-make-middle-healthy